READY TO LEARN

First Grade

Reading
Workbook

Table of Contents

"I see a big star in the sky." I said. "I see a lot of stars," said Max.

First grade is when children can bloom into readers by following simple strategies to help them use the sight words and letter-and-sound knowledge that they learned in kindergarten. Taking these skills to the next level will take practice, but practice can be fun! Help your child through the activities in this book and watch him or her grow into a successful reader.

What Good Readers Do:

1. Read every day.

2. Read everything around them.

3. Choose "just right" books.

4. Use strategies to help with words they don't know.

5. Think about what they read.

6. Make connections to what they read.

7. Make predictions about what they read.

8. Ask questions when they read.

Good readers read every day and read everything around them. There is so much to read! There are letters, numbers, words, signs, posters, books, grocery lists, and so much more. Protect your reading time. It is important to read, read, read every day!

Reading is fun and the stories you read can take you on amazing adventures. There are...

3 Ways to Read a Book

• Read the words.

• Look at the pictures to help you figure out the words.

• Retell what you read to a friend.

What is your favorite book? Write the title on the lines below.

_____

_____

_____

Go get that favorite book and have fun reading!

Choosing a Book That Is "Just Right" for You

Books are like shoes. Not everyone can wear the same size shoes. Make sure the book you are reading is not too difficult or too easy to read. Follow these simple steps to choose a book that is the right fit for you.

Use the five finger rule to help choose a just right book.

Five Finger Rule

Choose a book. Open it to any page.
Put one finger up for each
word you don't know.

0-1 fingers	Too easy
2-3 fingers	Just right
4 fingers	Give it a try
5+ fingers	Too hard

Decoding Strategies

A word is missing in each sentence below. Read the sentences and use the pictures as clues to help you decide what each missing word is. Circle the correct missing word and write it on the lines below.

The cat is up the _____.
(tree or top)

The boy has a _____.
(shoe or sandwich)

I like to play _____.
(baseball or soccer)

My mom likes to _____.
(cook or jump)

She is riding the _____.
(bus or bike)

Picture Clues

A word is missing in each sentence below. Read the sentences and use the pictures as clues to help you decide what each missing word is. Circle the correct missing word and write it on the lines below.

_____

I saw _____ at the zoo.
(fish or animals)

I saw _____ at the farm.
(pigs or lions)

I had an _____ for lunch.
(orange or apple)

I take the _____ to school.
(bus or canoe)

I had a birthday _____.
(chair or cake)

Initial Sounds

Look at the pictures. Write the missing letters to complete the words below.
Then read the words.

_____oy

_____un

_____ig

_____aby

_____able

_____at

_____etter

_____rog

_____oat

Decoding Strategies

Initial Sounds

Read the words in the pictures below.

Color the flowers with words that begin with the letter j.

Color the balloons with words that begin with the letter b.

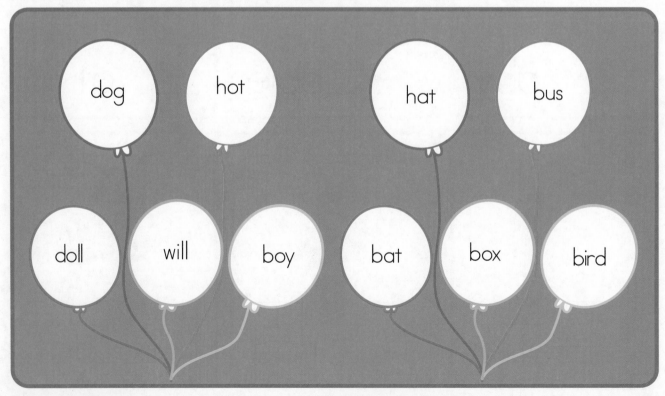

Decoding Strategies

Medial Sounds

Look at the pictures. Write the missing letters to complete the words below.

b___d

h___t

h___n

c___t

n___t

l___g

s___n

t___p

b___s

Medial Sounds

Write the missing vowels to complete each word below. Then draw a line to match the object on the left to its opposite on the right.

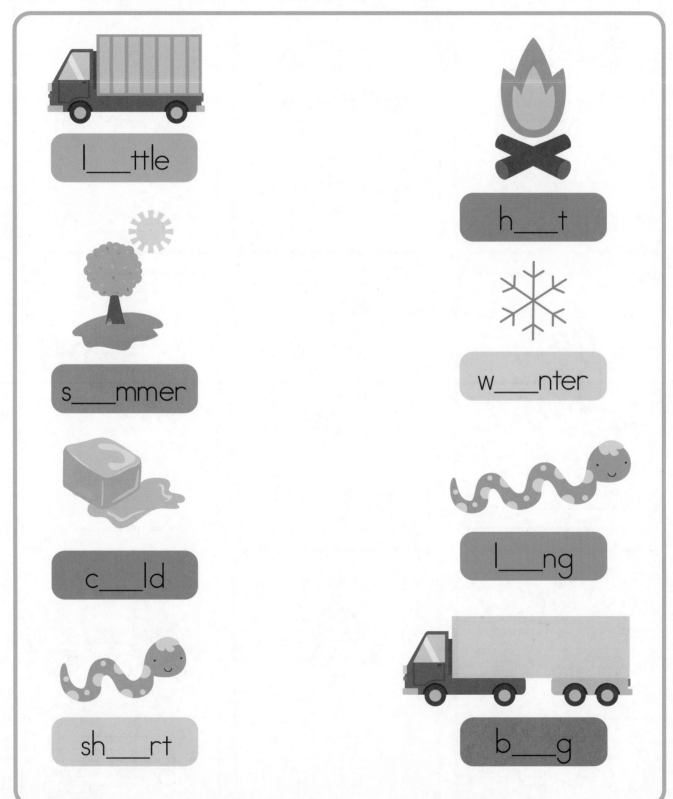

l___ttle

h___t

s___mmer

w___nter

c___ld

l___ng

sh___rt

b___g

Looking for "Chunks"

Some chunks are called rimes or word families because the words will rhyme.
Write a letter on each line below to create a word family. Color the snakes.

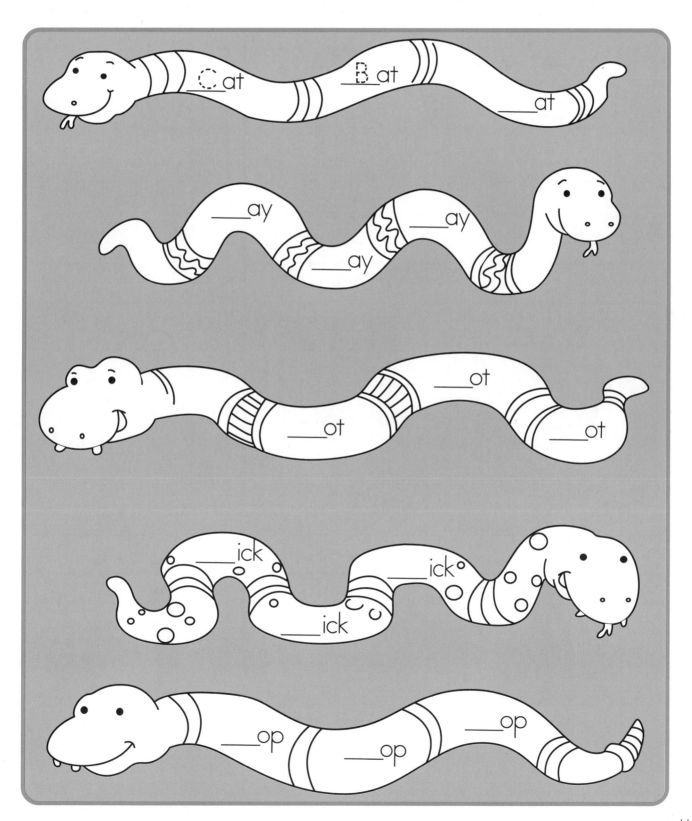

_C_at   _B_at   ___at

___ay   ___ay   ___ay

___ot   ___ot   ___ot

___ick   ___ick   ___ick

___op   ___op   ___op

Final Sounds with Double Consonants

Some words end with two of the same letter. Look at the pictures and complete the words by writing the missing double consonants on the lines below.

be_____

do_____

e_____

ba_____

wa_____

a_____

gra_____

dre_____

pu_____

Decoding Strategies

Looking for "Chunks"

Recognizing parts of words can help you sound out words faster. Look for "chunks" in the words you read.

Circle the words below that have the chunk shown on the left.

sh	share	chick	show
ch	chip	chin	this
th	that	when	there
at	shop	mat	bat
an	man	tan	cat
ack	rack	barn	sack
ip	top	sip	slip
ill	bill	fill	fall
op	mop	him	stop
ut	hut	hit	nut

Flipping the Vowel

Long Vowel Sounds

Write the missing vowels to complete each story. Then read the stories.

Come out to pl___y.

It is a sunny d___y.

What do you s___y?

I grew out of my tr___ke.

I now have a b___ke.

It is what I l___ke.

Decoding Strategies

Context Clues and Picture Clues

Sometimes trying to figure out a word by sounding it out may not help you. If this happens, try skipping the word and reading the rest of the sentence to see if you can figure out the word. Does the sentence sound right? Does it make sense? Another clue to help you figure out an unknown word is to look at the pictures on the page you are reading.

A word is missing in each sentence below. Read the sentences. Use the other words in the sentences and the pictures to help you figure out the missing words. Write the missing words on the lines below.

The _____ is on the log.

I can ride a _____ .

I see a cow near the _____ .

The cat has a red _____ .

I can climb a _____ .

Sight Words

Words to Practice and Know

There are some words that are difficult to sound out and that do not have picture clues. Reading and remembering them can make reading easier. Practice reading these sight words until you recognize them when you see them in books.

the	no	look	came
is	like	so	down
in	my	do	them
it	what	she	would
to	were	an	could
I	when	said	went
he	come	can	her
at	have	not	am
be	some	but	get
we	into	up	want

all	his	here	your
had	as	little	did
saw	on	make	about
this	for	yes	many
they	see	then	look
with	you	out	very
are	a	will	has
was	and	go	from
that	of	if	use
by	or	there	first

Sight Word Activities

Sight Words

Find and circle the sight words below using different colors for each word. Then fill in the graph by coloring one box for every sight word you find. Write the total number of words you find next to the graph on the lines below.

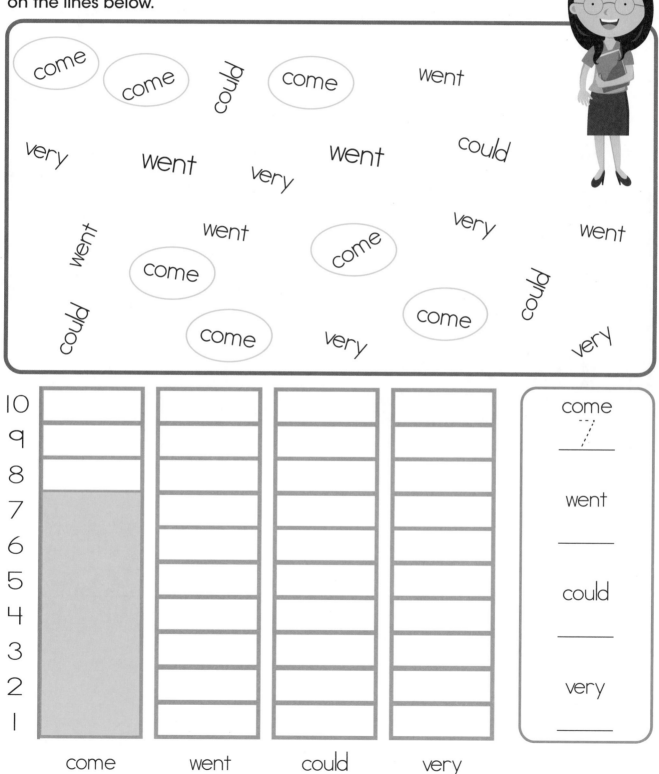

Sight Word Activities

Sight Words

Color the pumpkins below using the key.

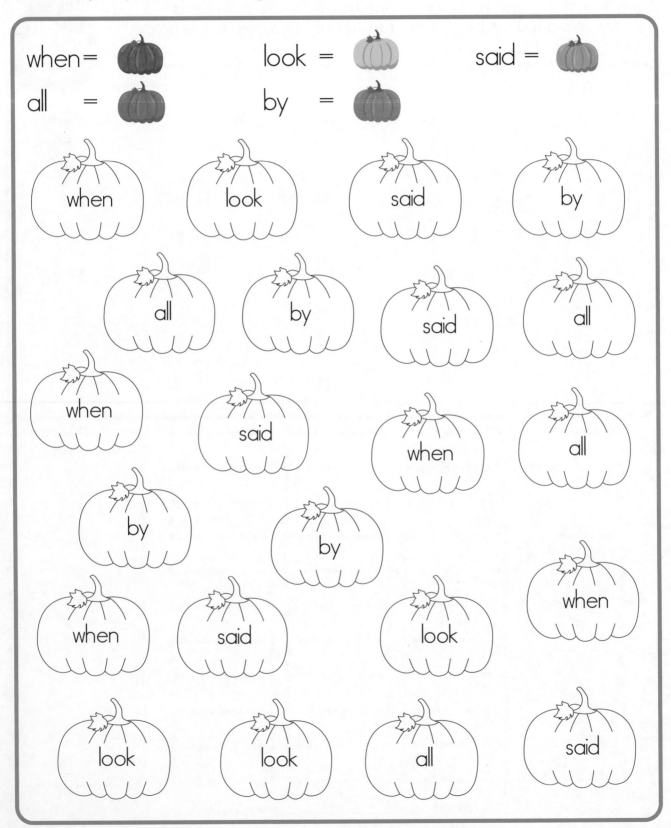

when = 🎃
look = 🎃
said = 🎃
all = 🎃
by = 🎃

when   look   said   by

all   by   said   all

when   said   when   all

by   by

when   said   look   when

look   look   all   said

Sight Words

Color the picture below using the key.

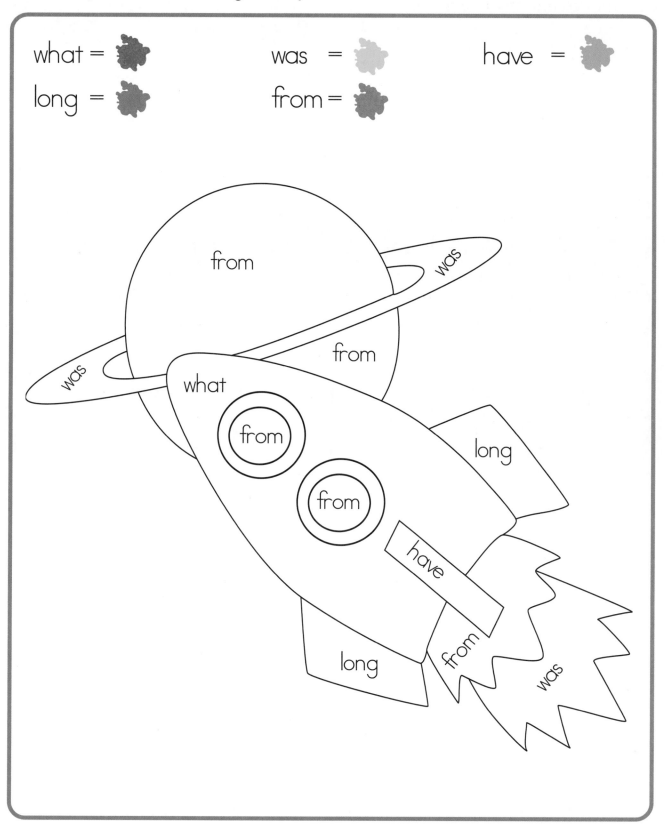

what = long =

was =

from =

have =

Sight Words

Roll a die and use the key to write the corresponding sight word in the correct column. Roll until the grid is full.

| saw | this | they | with | like | down |

Roll a Sight Word

Sight Word Activities

Sight Words

Complete the word search below by finding and circling all the sight words listed in the box. Words may be horizontal, vertical, or diagonal, but they will all be forwards—no backwards words allowed!

Search for the following words:

and	out	make	in	it
my	she	about	this	if

O	E	H	K	T	H	I	S	C	H	K
U	B	C	G	A	G	P	G	R	I	M
T	C	B	A	H	K	B	O	N	C	N
F	D	C	G	M	J	I	T	A	L	C
I	B	H	A	E	A	P	S	W	A	X
H	E	T	N	Z	B	K	C	V	F	U
O	M	E	D	F	R	S	E	N	K	E
F	B	F	G	P	Q	H	M	A	L	G
N	R	A	N	J	O	E	D	I	G	J
O	A	W	L	G	S	I	F	X	Y	Z
M	Y	I	J	Q	B	K	O	F	C	Y
O	A	B	O	U	T	F	L	E	I	X

Sight Words and Strategies

Read the sentences below. The sight words are underlined. Use the reading strategies you have learned to read the other words.

He can sip from the cup.

I like my red shoes.

The cat is not fat.

The dog ran home.

Sight Words and Strategies

Read the sentences below. The sight words are underlined. Use the reading strategies you have learned to read the other words.

How many cats do you see?

She loves jumping rope.

I have a pet goat.

The frog is on the log.

Rhymes and Rhyming Words

Words That Rhyme

Words that rhyme have the same ending sound. Circle the words that rhyme.
Then color the pictures.

Take my hand
and we will sit on the sand,
while we hear the best band
in all of the land.

Hooray! Hooray!
What a beautiful day.
We can swim in the bay,
and catch a sun ray.

Words That Rhyme

Circle the words that rhyme. Then color the picture.

Oh rats! I just saw three cats
wearing three aprons
and three floppy hats!

What a funny sight!
These dogs like to write,
but only at night.
Are you sure that is right?

Word Meanings

Read the story below.

Halloween Night

It was raining on Halloween night. I was feeling disappointed. I had a great monster costume. I got dressed up anyway. I jumped out and surprised my dad and frightened him. Finally, the rain stopped and my dad took me trick-or-treating.

Read the questions below about the story and circle the correct answers.

In the story, the word "disappointed" means:

a. scared   **b.** happy   **c.** sad

The word "frightened" means:

a. happy   **b.** scared   **c.** sad

The word "finally" means:

a. at last   **b.** first   **c.** before

Vocabulary

Word Meanings

Read the story below.

The Circus

I can't believe it happened! I was at the circus with my mom. A tiger let out a huge roar. The magician was doing tricks. Then a clown picked me out of the audience to help. The magician made me disappear!

Read the questions below about the story and circle the correct answers.

In the story, the word "huge" means:

a. small　　　　　　　b. very big　　　　　　　c. tiny

The word "audience" means:

a. a loud noise　　　　b. people watching a show　c. tired

The word "disappear" means:

a. turn purple　　　　b. can't be seen　　　　c. get really hungry

Word Meanings

Read the story below.

Our New Car

My mom got a new car. The paint is crimson. She uses the vacuum every day to keep it clean. She is really proud of her new car.

Read the questions below about the story and circle the correct answers.

The word "crimson" means:

a. shiny   b. red   c. big

The word "vacuum" means:

a. a cleaning tool   b. a toy   c. a pet

The word "proud" means:

a. feeling happy   b. feeling sad   c. feeling afraid

The Cover

The cover is an important part of a book. It is the first thing a reader sees. It helps the reader decide if he or she is interested in the book.

Use the information above to answer the questions. Write your answers on the lines below.

What is the book about?

_____

_____

Who drew the pictures in the book?

_____

_____

Who wrote the words in the book?

_____

_____

Text and Illustrations

The inside of books can look different. Some books have pictures and others just have words. Most of the books read in first grade have both!

"I see a big star in the sky," I said.

"I see a lot of stars," said Max.

Text
The words in the book that tell the story

Illustration
The picture helps readers understand what the sentences are saying or explaining.

Use the picture and sentences in the book to answer the questions. Write your answers on the lines below.

Is it daytime or nighttime? How do you know?

_____

_____

_____

_____

_____

_____

_____

_____

_____

_____

Reading Elements

Characters

Characters **are the** people, animals, **or** other creatures **in the story.**

Color the characters in the picture below.

Setting

The setting is where a story takes place.

Look at the pictures. Then draw a line from the picture to the name of the setting.

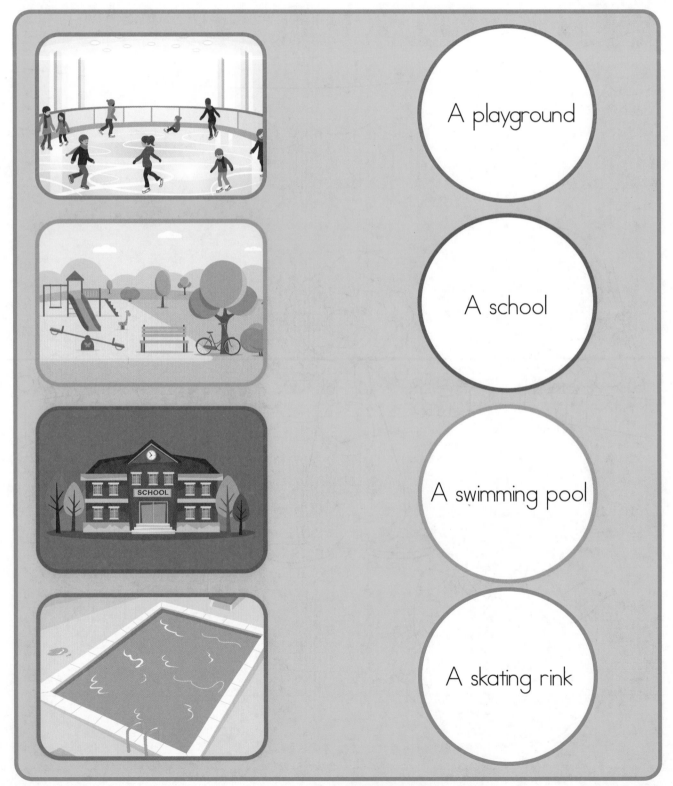

Reading Elements

Problem and Solution

The problem in a story is something that happens that needs to be fixed.
The solution in a story is how the problem is solved.

Look at the picture and use your reading strategies to read the sentences and answer the questions. Write your answers on the lines below.

Kristin and Zac wanted macaroni and cheese for dinner. When they started cooking, they didn't have any cheese. Mom went to the store to get some. They all had macaroni and cheese for dinner that night.

What is the problem in the story?

_____

_____

_____

_____

_____

What is the solution?

_____

_____

_____

_____

_____

Problem and Solution

Read the problems below and draw a line to the picture that shows the solution.

Pat missed the bus.

Liam forgot his lunch at home.

Sammy keeps tripping on her shoelaces.

Lucas spilled his glass of milk.

Maya fell and scraped her knee.

Sequencing

Read the story below.

At the Park

I went to play with my friend at the park. We played on the slide. We played tag. We played on the swings. We had so much fun at the park.

Draw a line from the picture to the order the event happens in the story.

First — What happened in the beginning of the story

Next — What happened next in the story

Then — Then what happened in the story

Last — What happened at the end of the story

Sequencing

Read the story below.

Maggie's Day Out

Hi! My name is Maggie. I am a dog. The other day I left my house and went for a run. I saw a cat and chased it down the street. When I got hungry, I went home for dinner. What a great day!

Draw a line from the illustrations to the order of events in the story.

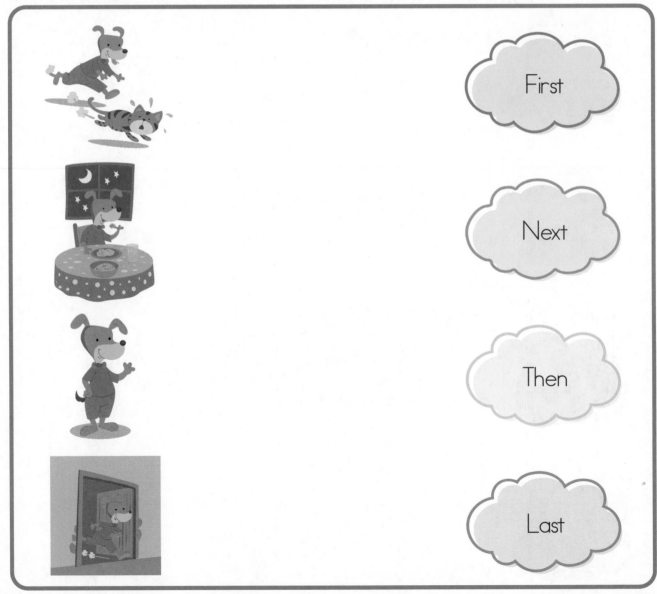

First

Next

Then

Last

Sequencing

Read the story below.

The Big Ship

The big ship is anchored to the dock. Machines unload big metal boxes onto trucks. The ship blows its loud horn. Then the big ship pulls away from the dock.

Draw a line from the illustrations to the order of events in the story.

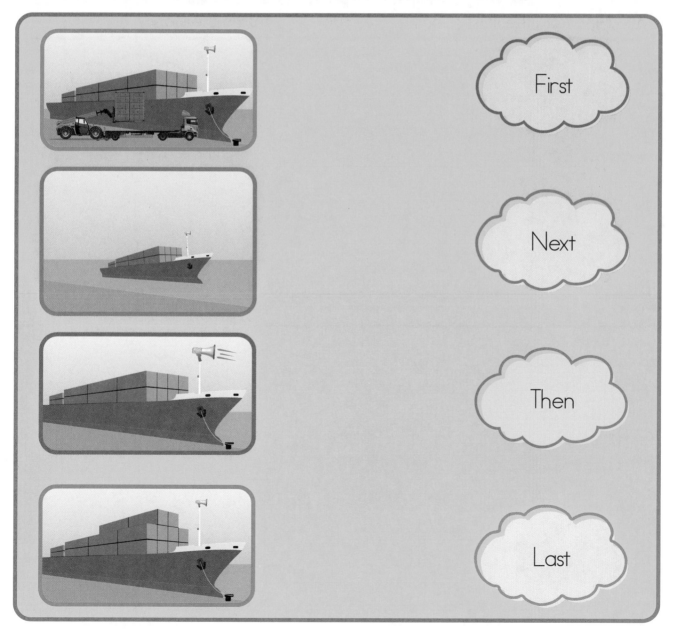

First

Next

Then

Last

Sequencing

Read the story below.

Making a Cake

I made a cake today! My mom and I mixed the batter in a bowl. I licked the spoon. We poured the batter in a cake pan and put it in the oven. When it was done, we put icing on the cake. It was delicious. YUM!

Draw a line from the illustrations to the order of events in the story.

First

Next

Then

Last

The cover of a book can help you predict what the book is about.

My Loose Tooth

Written by
Joe Fitzpatrick
Illustrated by
Skylar Everett

- The title and the illustration give you a hint.
- The author's name might even give you a hint if you have read a book written by them before.

Use the information above to predict what this book is about. Write your answer on the lines below.

The book is about...

Making Predictions

Use the cover to make predictions about the book. Draw a line from the book cover to your prediction.

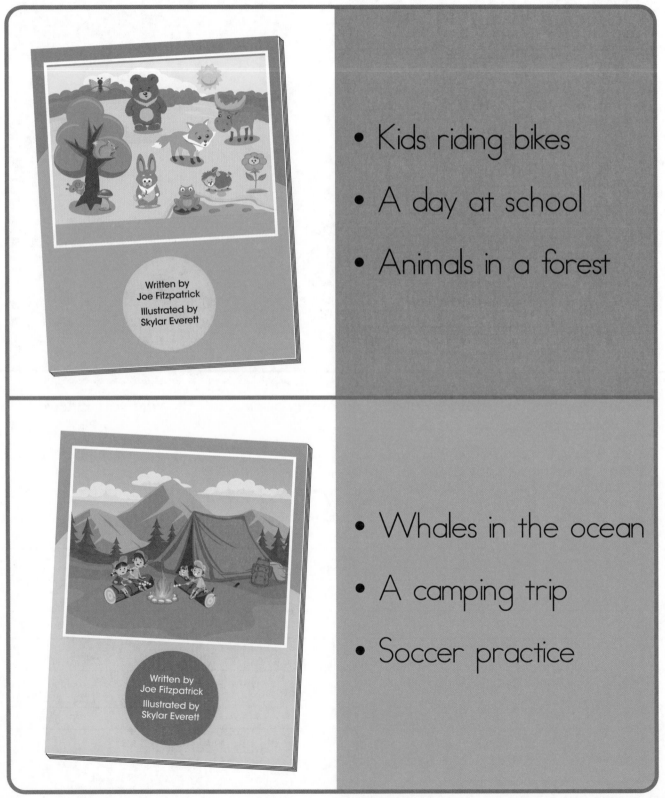

- Kids riding bikes

- A day at school

- Animals in a forest

- Whales in the ocean

- A camping trip

- Soccer practice

Making Predictions

Make predictions as you read.

Read the story below.

The Triple Cactus

Zac was riding his skateboard. He was doing lots of tricks. Zac was great at doing tricks. He decided to try one he had never done before. It was called the triple cactus.

On the lines below, write what you think will happen next.

_____

_____

_____

_____

_____

_____

_____

_____

Visualizing What You Read

Reading a story can paint a picture in your mind. Close your eyes and think about a birthday cake. Do you have a picture in your mind of what it looks like? That is visualizing!

Read the sentences below and draw a picture of what you imagine.

It is my birthday.
I cannot wait for my party!

Reading Comprehension

Visualizing What You Read

Read the sentences below and draw a picture of what you imagine.

My dad is taking me to the game
this weekend. I am so excited!

Visualizing What You Read

Read the sentence below and draw a picture of what you imagine.

Tomorrow we go on vacation!

Reading Comprehension

Visualizing What You Read

Read the sentence below and draw a picture of what you imagine.

We got our first family pet today.

Reading Comprehension

Making Connections

When something in a story reminds you of something that happened to you, you are making a connection to the story!

Read the story below.

The Loose Tooth

I had an apple for lunch today. When I bit into my apple, I felt something pop. I moved my tongue around in my mouth and felt a loose tooth! I wiggled it all day long thinking it would come out, but it didn't. When I got home, I showed my mom and she had an idea.

Do you feel a connection to the story? Have you ever had a loose tooth? Write about it on the lines below.

_____

_____

_____

_____

_____

_____

_____

_____

_____

_____

Making Connections

Read the story below.

Melissa and the Three Bunnies

One day, Melissa was walking in the forest when she saw a little house. She decided to go in to see who was home. On the table she saw three carrots. She was very hungry and decided to eat one. The big carrot was too hot. The small carrot was too cold. The medium carrot was just right.

Do you feel a connection to the story? Does this story remind you of any other stories you have read? Have you ever been very hungry? Write about it on the lines below.

_____

_____

_____

_____

_____

_____

_____

_____

_____

_____

Reading Comprehension

Understanding What You Read Using Clues

Look at each picture and read the sentences. Circle the sentence that matches the picture and then write it on the lines below.

The boy is making a cake.
The girl is painting the fence.

_____

_____

The farmer is milking the cow.
The man is chopping down the tree.

_____

_____

The pig is in the barn.
The horse jumped over the fence.

_____

_____

The girl is reading a book.
The boys are playing tag.

_____

_____

Reading Comprehension

Understanding What You Read Using Clues

Use the clues to find out who each character is. Draw a line from the character to his or her name.

Connor is wearing a red shirt. He likes to play soccer.

Gabby plays with her baby doll.

Max loves to read.

Kate loves to pick flowers.

Max

Gabby

Kate

Connor

Reading Comprehension

Understanding What You Read Using Clues

Read the sentences and color the picture that matches the clues.

I walk sideways.

I have claws.

I love to go for walks and play fetch.

I have four legs.

I live on a farm.

I make milk.

I love to eat carrots.

I have long ears.

Reading Comprehension

Understanding What You Read Using Clues

Read the sentences below.

Hannah is wearing a pink top. Jane is wearing a green skirt with a green top. Jane always wears a bow in her hair to match her top. Ben has curly hair and is wearing a blue sweater and blue jeans. Kurt has brown hair and it is the same color as his jacket. Jacob has red hair that matches his favorite shoes.

Color the picture to match the sentences. Then, on the lines below, answer the questions about what you read.

How many kids are waiting for the school bus?_____

Who is first in line?_____

Who is last in line?_____

Following Directions

Read the directions below and color the picture.

1. Color the bush to the left of the house green.
2. Color the sun yellow.
3. Color the chimney on the roof red.
4. Color the windows light blue.
5. Draw some fluffy clouds in the sky.
6. Draw three flowers near the tree.
7. Color the door red.
8. Color the leaves on the tree green.
9. Color the rest of the house any color you like.

Following Directions

Read the sentences below and complete the picture.

1. Draw a beach umbrella for the family.
2. Draw a boat on the water.
3. Draw a sun in the sky.
4. Draw a kite in the sky.
5. Draw a crab on the sand.
6. Draw a pail and shovel on the beach.
7. Draw a beach ball.
8. Draw yourself on the beach.

Seasons

Read the poem below. Then color the pictures.

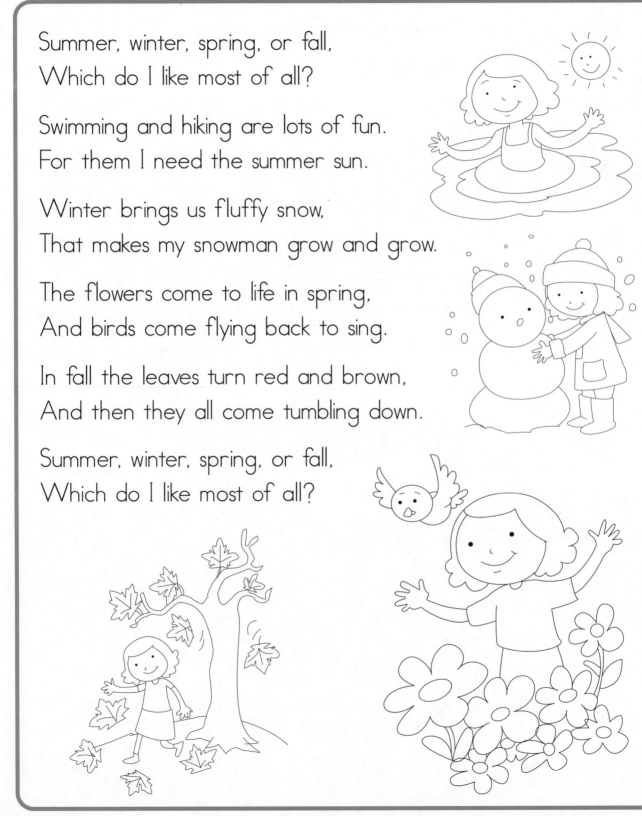

Summer, winter, spring, or fall,
Which do I like most of all?

Swimming and hiking are lots of fun.
For them I need the summer sun.

Winter brings us fluffy snow,
That makes my snowman grow and grow.

The flowers come to life in spring,
And birds come flying back to sing.

In fall the leaves turn red and brown,
And then they all come tumbling down.

Summer, winter, spring, or fall,
Which do I like most of all?

Climbing Trees

Read the story below. Then color the picture.

Ella and Finn like to climb trees. They see a kitten in the tree. The kitten is afraid. It will not come down. Finn tries to help the kitten. The kitten climbs higher up the tree. Ella pats the kitten and picks it up. Finn and Ella are good climbers. They are good helpers, too!

Comic Strip Fun

Read the comic strip below.

Soccer

Read the story below. Then color the picture.

Hector is going to play soccer today.

He is very happy.

He likes to play soccer.

After the game begins, it starts to rain.

The kids keep playing anyway.

It got very muddy! It was a lot of fun!

Riddles

Riddles **are** brain teasers **that make you think. Read the riddles below and try to answer them. Then color the pictures.**

1. I am full of holes, but I can still hold water.
   What am I?_____

2. I have hands and a face, but I can't touch or smile.
   What am I? _____

3. I get wetter and wetter the more I dry.
   What am I? _____

4. I have lots of keys but can't open any door.
   What am I? _____

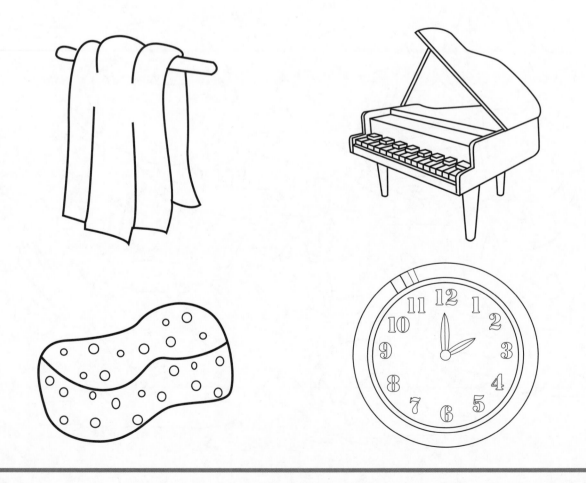

Compound Words

Compound words **are** two words that make a new word when they are put together. **Look at the pictures to figure out the compound words. Write the words on the lines below.**

football

=

=

=

=

ANSWER KEY

Page 5

Decoding Strategies

Look at the Pictures

A word is missing in each sentence below. Read the sentences and use the pictures as clues to help you decide what each missing word is. Circle the correct missing word and write it on the lines below.

The cat is up the **tree**
(tree or top)

The boy has a **sandwich**
(shoe or sandwich)

I like to play **soccer**
(baseball or soccer)

My mom likes to **cook**
(cook or jump)

She is riding the **bike**
(bus or bike)

5

Page 6

Decoding Strategies

Picture Clues

A word is missing in each sentence below. Read the sentences and use the pictures as clues to help you decide what each missing word is. Circle the correct missing word and write it on the lines below.

I saw **animals** at the zoo.
(fish or animals)

I saw **pigs** at the farm.
(pigs or lions)

I had an **apple** for lunch.
(orange or apple)

I take the **bus** to school.
(bus or canoe)

I had a birthday **cake**.
(chair or cake)

6

Page 7

Decoding Strategies

Initial Sounds

Look at the pictures. Write the missing letters to complete the words below. Then read the words.

b_oy r_un p_ig

b_aby t_able c_at

l_etter f_rog g_oat

7

Page 8

Decoding Strategies

Initial Sounds

Read the words in the pictures below.
Color the flowers with words that begin with the letter j.

cat, jump, joy, dog, just, job, mat, milk, bat, jar

Color the balloons with words that begin with the letter b.

dog, hot, hat, bus, doll, dd, boy, bat, box, bird

8

Page 9

Decoding Strategies

Medial Sounds

Look at the pictures. Write the missing letters to complete the words below.

b_e_d h_a_t h_e_n

c_a_t n_e_t l_o_g

s_u_n t_o_p b_u_s

9

Page 10

Decoding Strategies

Medial Sounds

Write the missing vowels to complete each word below. Then draw a line to match the object on the left to its opposite on the right.

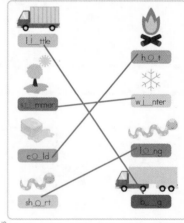

li_ttle h_o_t
s_u_mmer w_i_nter
c_o_ld l_o_ng
sh_o_rt b_i_g

10

Page 12

Decoding Strategies

Final Sounds with Double Consonants

Some words end with two of the same letter. Look at the pictures and complete the words by writing the missing double consonants on the lines below.

be_l_l do_l_l e_g_g

ba_l_l wa_l_l a_d_d

gra_s_s dre_s_s pu_l_l

12

Page 13

Decoding Strategies

Looking for "Chunks"

Recognizing parts of words can help you sound out words faster. Look for "chunks" in the words you read.
Circle the words below that have the chunk shown on the left.

sh	(share)	chick	(show)
ch	(chip)	(chin)	this
th	(that)	when	(there)
at	shop	(mat)	(bat)
an	(man)	(tan)	cat
ack	(rack)	barn	(sack)
ip	top	(sip)	(slip)
ill	(bill)	(fill)	fall
op	(mop)	him	(stop)
ut	(hut)	hit	(nut)

13

Page 14

Decoding Strategies

Flipping the Vowel
Long Vowel Sounds

Write the missing vowels to complete each story. Then read the stories.

Come out to pl_a_y.

It is a sunny d_a_y.

What do you s_a_y?

I grew out of my tr_i_ke.

I now have a b_i_ke.

It is what I l_i_ke.

14

60

Decoding Strategies

Context Clues and Picture Clues
Sometimes trying to figure out a word by sounding it out may not help you. If this happens, try skipping the word and reading the rest of the sentence to see if you can figure out the word. Does the sentence sound right? Does it make sense? Another clue to help you figure out an unknown word is to look at the pictures on the page you are reading.

A word is missing in each sentence below. Read the sentences. Use the other words in the sentences and the pictures to help you figure out the missing words. Write the missing words on the lines below.

The __frog__ is on the log.

I can ride a __bike__

I see a cow near the __barn__

The cat has a red __hat__

I can climb a __tree__

15

Sight Word Activities

Sight Words
Find and circle the sight words below using different colors for each word. Then fill in the graph by coloring one box for every sight word you find. Write the total number of words you find next to the graph on the lines below.

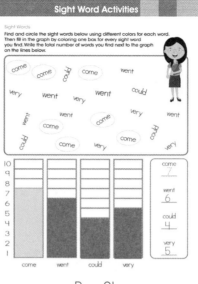

come	7
went	6
could	4
very	5

Sight Word Activities

Sight Words
Color the pumpkins below using the key.

when =   look =   said =
all =   by =

18

Sight Word Activities

Sight Words
Color the picture below using the key.

what =   was =   have =
long =   from =

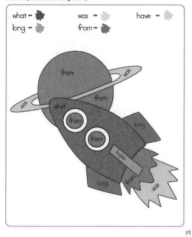

19

Sight Word Activities

Sight Words
Complete the word search below by finding and circling all the sight words listed in the box. Words may be horizontal, vertical, or diagonal, but they will all be forwards—no backwards words allowed! Search for the following words:

| and | out | make | in | it |
| my | she | about | this | if |

O	E	H	K	T	H	I	S	C	H	K
U	B	C	G	A	G	P	G	R	I	M
T	C	B	A	H	K	B	O	N	C	N
F	D	C	G	M	J	I	T	A	L	C
I	B	H	A	E	A	P	S	W	A	X
H	E	T	N	Z	B	K	C	V	F	U
O	M	E	D	F	R	S	E	N	K	E
F	B	F	G	P	Q	H	M	A	L	G
N	R	A	N	J	O	E	D	I	G	J
O	A	W	L	G	S	I	F	X	Y	Z
M	Y	I	J	Q	B	K	O	F	C	Y
O	A	B	O	U	T	F	L	E	I	X

Rhymes and Rhyming Words

Words That Rhyme
Words that rhyme have the same ending sound. Circle the words that rhyme. Then color the pictures.

Take my hand
and we will sit on the sand
while we hear the best band
in all of the land.

Hooray! Hooray!
What a beautiful day.
We can swim in the bay
and catch a sun ray.

24

Rhymes and Rhyming Words

Words That Rhyme
Circle the words that rhyme. Then color the picture.

What a funny sight!
These dogs like to write
but only at night.
Are you sure that it right?

25

Vocabulary

Word Meanings
Read the story below.

Halloween Night
It was raining on Halloween night. I was feeling disappointed. I had a great monster costume. I got dressed up anyway. I jumped out and surprised my dad and frightened him. Finally the rain stopped and my dad took me trick-or-treating.

Read the questions below about the story and circle the correct answers.
In the story, the word "disappointed" means:
a. scared   b. happy   **c. sad**

The word "frightened" means:
a. happy   **b. scared**   c. sad

The word "finally" means:
a. at last   b. first   c. before

26

Vocabulary

Word Meanings
Read the story below.

The Circus
I can't believe it happened! I was at the circus with my mom. A tiger let out a huge roar. The magician was doing tricks. Then a clown picked me out of the audience to help. The magician made me disappear!

Read the questions below about the story and circle the correct answers.
In the story, the word "huge" means:
a. small   **b. very big**   c. tiny

The word "audience" means:
a. a loud noise   **b. people watching a show**   c. tired

The word "disappear" means:
a. turn purple   **b. can't be seen**   c. get really hungry

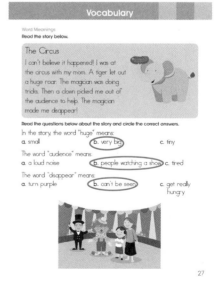

27

Page 28

Word Meanings
Read the story below.

Our New Car

My mom got a new car. The paint is crimson. She uses the vacuum every day to keep it clean. She is really proud of her new car.

Read the questions below about the story and circle the correct answers.

The word "crimson" means:
a. shiny   (b. red)   c. big

The word "vacuum" means:
(a. a cleaning tool)   b. a toy   c. a pet

The word "proud" means:
(a. feeling happy)   b. feeling sad   c. feeling afraid

28

Page 29

The Cover
The cover is an important part of a book. It is the first thing a reader sees. It helps the reader decide if he or she is interested in the book.

Use the information above to answer the questions. Write your answers on the lines below.
What is the book about?

My first sleepover

Who drew the pictures in the book?

Skylar Everett

Who wrote the words in the book?

Joe Fitzpatrick

29

Page 32

Setting
The setting is where the story takes place.

Look at the pictures. Then draw a line from the picture to the name of the setting.

A playground

A school

A swimming pool

A skating rink

32

Page 33

Problem and Solution
The problem in the story is something that happens that needs to be fixed. The solution in the story is how the problem is solved.

Look at the picture and use your reading strategies to read the sentences and answer the questions. Write your answers on the lines below.

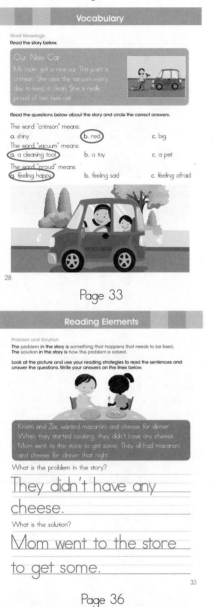

Kristin and Zac wanted macaroni and cheese for dinner. When they started cooking, they didn't have any cheese. Mom went to the store to get some. They all had macaroni and cheese for dinner that night.

What is the problem in the story?

They didn't have any cheese.

What is the solution?

Mom went to the store to get some.

33

Page 34

Problem and Solution
Read the problems below and draw a line to the picture of the solution.

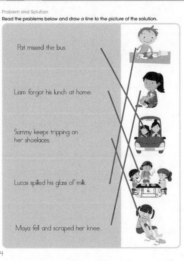

Pat missed the bus.

Liam forgot his lunch at home.

Sammy keeps tripping on her shoelaces.

Lucas spilled his glass of milk.

Maya fell and scraped her knee.

34

Page 35

Sequencing
Read the story below.

At the Park

I went to play with my friend at the park. We played on the slide. We played tag. We played on the swings. We had so much fun at the park.

Draw a line from the picture to the order the event happens in the story.

First — What happened in the beginning of the story

Next — What happened next in the story

Then — Then what happened in the story

Last — What happened at the end of the story

35

Page 36

Sequencing
Read the story below.

Maggie's Day Out

Hi! My name is Maggie. I am a dog. The other day I left my house and went for a run. I saw a cat and chased it down the street. When I got hungry, I went home for dinner. What a great day!

Draw a line from the illustrations to the order of events in the story.

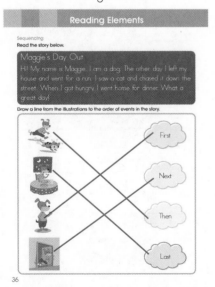

First

Next

Then

Last

36

Page 37

Sequencing
Read the story below.

The Big Ship

The big ship is anchored to the dock. Machines unload big metal boxes onto trucks. The ship blows its loud horn. Then the big ship pulls away from the dock.

Draw a line from the illustrations to the order of events in the story.

First

Next

Then

Last

37

Page 38

Sequencing
Read the story below.

Making a Cake

I made a cake today! My mom and I mixed the batter in a bowl. I licked the spoon. We poured the batter in a cake pan and put it in the oven. When it was done, we put icing on the cake. It was delicious. YUM!

Draw a line from the illustrations to the order of events in the story.

First

Next

Then

Last

38

Page 40

Making Predictions
Use the cover to make predictions about the book. Draw a line from the book cover to your prediction.

- Kids riding bikes
- A day at school
- Animals in a forest

- Whales in the ocean
- A camping trip
- Soccer practice

40

Page 48

Understanding What You Read Using Clues
Look at each picture and read the sentences. Circle the sentence that matches the picture and then rewrite it on the lines below.

The boy is making a cake.
The girl is painting the fence.

The girl is painting the fence.

The farmer is milking the cow.
The man is chopping down the tree.

The farmer is milking the cow.

The pig is in the barn.
The horse jumped over the fence.

The pig is in the barn.

The girl is reading a book.
The boys are playing tag.

The boys are playing tag.

48

Page 49

Understanding What You Read Using Clues
Use the clues to find out who each character is. Draw a line from the character to his or her name.

Connor is wearing a red shirt. He likes to play soccer.
Gabby plays with her baby doll.
Max loves to read.
Kate loves to pick flowers.

Max
Gabby
Kate
Connor

49

Page 50

Understanding What You Read Using Clues
Read the sentences and color the picture that matches the clues.

I walk sideways.
I have claws.

I love to go for walks and play fetch.
I have four legs.

I live on a farm.
I make milk.

I love to eat carrots.
I have long ears.

50

Page 51

Understanding What You Read Using Clues
Read the sentences below.

Hannah is wearing a pink top. Jane is wearing a green skirt with a green top. Jane always wears a bow in her hair to match her top. Ben has curly hair and is wearing a blue sweater and blue jeans. Kurt has brown hair and it is the same color as his jacket. Jacob has red hair that matches his favorite shoes.

Color the picture to match the sentences. Then, on the lines below, answer the questions about what you read.
How many kids are waiting for the school bus? five
Who is first in line? Jacob
Who is last in line? Ben

51

Page 52

Following Directions
Read the directions below and color the picture.

1. Color the bush to the left of the house green.
2. Color the sun yellow.
3. Color the chimney on the roof red.
4. Color the windows light blue.
5. Draw some fluffy clouds in the sky.
6. Draw three flowers near the tree.
7. Color the door red.
8. Color the leaves on the tree green.
9. Color the rest of the house any color you like.

52

Page 58

Riddles
Riddles are brain teasers that make you think. Read the riddles below and try to answer them. Then, color the pictures.

1. I am full of holes, but I can still hold water.
   What am I? sponge
2. I have hands and a face, but I can't touch or smile.
   What am I? clock
3. I get wetter and wetter the more I dry.
   What am I? towel
4. I have lots of keys but can't open any door.
   What am I? piano

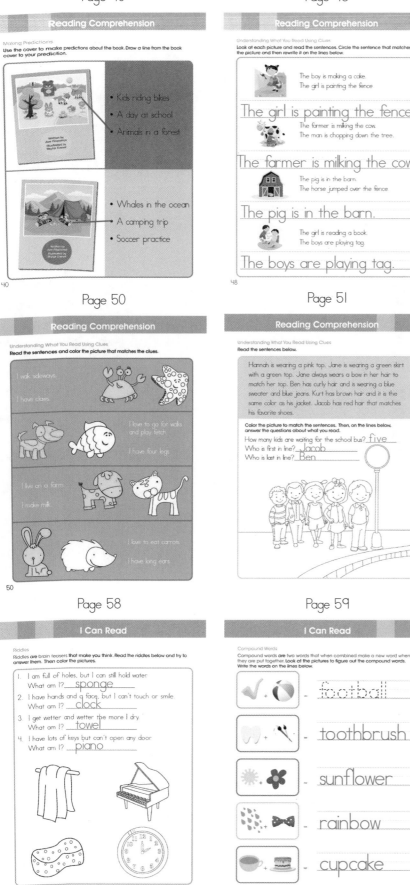

Page 59

Compound Words
Compound words are two words that when combined make a new word when they are put together. Look at the pictures to figure out the compound words. Write the words on the lines below.

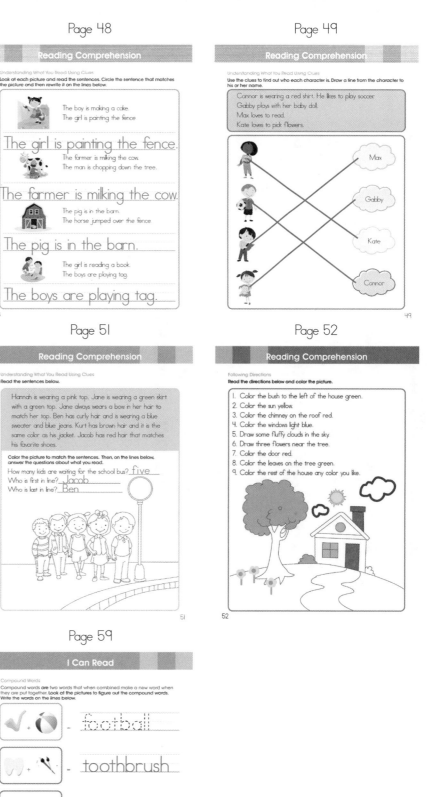

✓ + ○ = football

+ = toothbrush

+ = sunflower

+ = rainbow

+ = cupcake

59

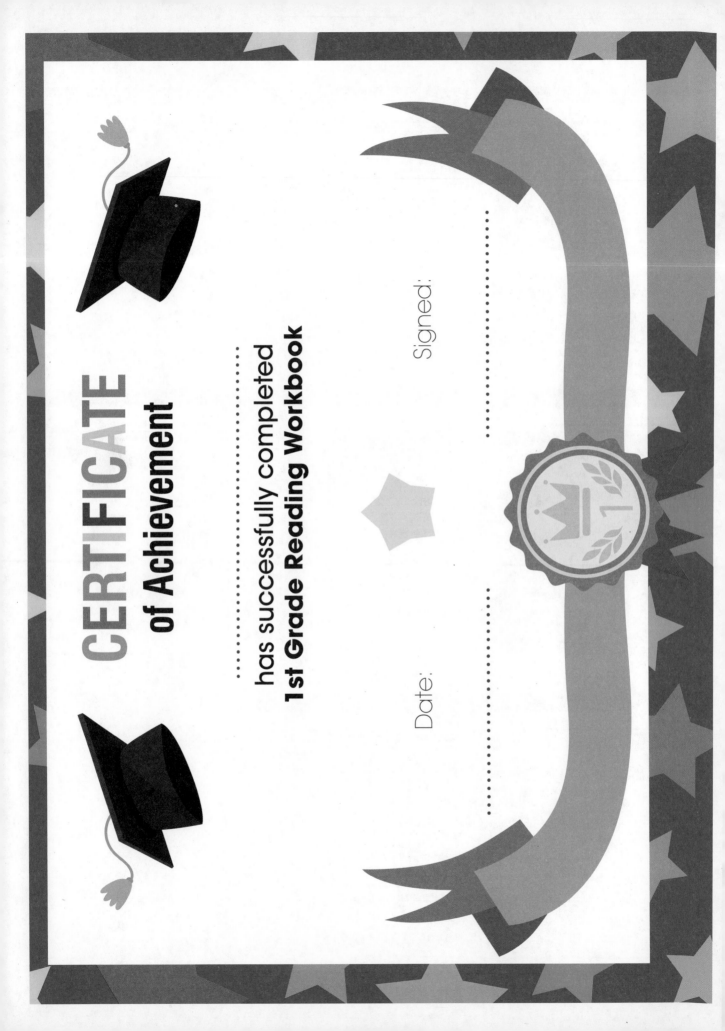

CERTIFICATE
of Achievement

....

has successfully completed
1st Grade Reading Workbook

Date:

Signed: